JAMES BRAMSTON

THE
ART *of* POLITICKS

(1729)

Introduction by
William Kinsley

I

For your free PDF copy of our latest catalog,

or to order a full color print version of our latest catalog,

please visit our website at

WWW.THEOPHANIA.CA.

Address all correspondence regarding editorial matters, advertising, commercial wholesale ordering, and all publishing queries to:

Theophania Publishing

1040-8th Ave SW, Calgary, AB

T2P 1J2, Canada.

Follow us on Twitter at:

@TheophaniaBooks

INTRODUCTION

The meagre information known about James Bramston's life has been ably summarized by F. P. Lock in his introduction to *The Man of Taste* (ARS 171). For our present purposes, we need only add that Bramston seems to have been acquainted with Pope, who saw *The Art of Politicks* before it was printed and thought it "pretty". Bramston quite likely met Pope through John Caryll, whose Sussex estate, Lady-Holt, was in the neighborhood of Bramston's parishes.

The Art of Politicks, Bramston's first English poem, was published anonymously in 1729 and advertised in the Monthly Chronicle of 8 December. Several reimpressions followed, as did another London edition, one from Edinburgh, and two from Dublin, all dated 1729, and a London edition of 1731. It was reprinted in Robert Dodsley's *Collection of Poems, by Several Hands* (1748), where it was attributed to Bramston, and in John Bell's *Classical Arrangement of Fugitive Poetry*, Volume 5 (1789), with a few notes. Horace Walpole's copy of Dodsley's *Collection*, with a few rather uninformative manuscript notes, is now in the British Library (C.117.aa.16).

It seems likely that the poem was completed in the summer of 1729. The most recent events that Bramston alludes to are Thomas Woolston's trial for blasphemy of 4 March (p. 27) and Sir Paul Methuen's resignation as Treasurer of the King's Household, which was reported in May (p. 13).

Horace's *Ars Poetica* was one of the most fertile sources for eighteenth-century imitations and adaptations. Some were completely serious attempts to marry one art to another or to show that all arts share the same fundamental principles; an example of this type is John Gwynn's *Art of Architecture* (1742; ARS 144). Others, like William King's *Art of Cookery* (1708) are downright burlesques.

Bramston's usual method falls somewhere between these extremes. He often uses the dignity of poetry to show up the indignity of politics or political writing, as on pp. 5-6 where Horace's advice on choice of subject is transformed into advice to "*Weekly Writers* of seditious *News*," or on page 7, where the rise and fall of South Sea stock fills the place of Horace's famous comparison of archaic and new-coined words to the leaves of the forest. But Bramston's poem more often aspires to the same level as its model; in this respect it resembles *Absalom and Achitophel* more than *Mac Flecknoe*.

Several factors help to bring *Ars Poetica* and *The Art of Politicks* together. Perhaps most important, Bramston conceives of politics primarily as a verbal art, the use of speech to persuade others to a course of action. Bribes and other crasser incentives appear in the poem, of course, but they are clearly the result of declining standards. For Bramston, rhetoric should govern politics; the House of Commons is a reincarnation of a Roman senate or courtroom. Bramston's inclusion of political writing as well as politics itself in his poem also helps to keep him in Horace's orbit. On Horace's side, his conception of poetry is basically rhetorical and persuasive; it should instruct and delight, move to laughter or tears. Horace's readiness to digress into literary history gives Bramston many opportunities to bring in political history. The *Ars Poetica* is very much concerned with the world of men; poets are seen in their social roles, and Horace's standards of literary decorum are usually based on social norms: young men in plays should behave the way young men are observed to behave in real life. The *Ars Poetica* also contains several sharp satiric darts; Horace's contrast between the eloquence of ancient Greece and the commercial arithmetic of modern Rome slides easily into a contrast between Elizabethan learning and Hanoverian place-hunting (pp.32-33). Finally, Horace's urbane and chatty style is as suitable for other subjects as it is for poetry. To appreciate Horace's adaptability, one need only imagine the difficulty of writing an art of politics in imitation of Archibald MacLeish's "Ars Poetica" or Aristotle's *Poetics*.

Though he does not pretend to Pope's image of himself as a new Horace bringing the whole weight of Roman tradition to bear on contemporary society, Bramston is very clever on the local level at transposing Horace for his own purposes. Horace recounts the increasing complexity and sophistication of theatrical music, Bramston the increasingly elaborated musical celebrations of victorious candidates (pp. 22-23), and Horace's implication that the sophistication of taste is really a decline—"an impetuous style brought in an unwonted diction" (217)—constitutes an unspoken comment on Bramston's subject. Bramston's page 27 corresponds to Horace's brief history of the theatre, from Thespis's tragedies that he staged on wagons to the silencing of the excessively outspoken chorus of Old Comedy (275-84). Bramston replaces Thespis with Defoe, and the wagon-mounted stage with the cart and pillory. Instead of deploring the silencing of the chorus, Bramston applauds the silencing of Woolston. The contrast between Thespis and Defoe is clearly mock-heroic, but Bramston implies that Woolston's similarity to an ancient satyr is a decline from the character expected of a modern clergyman.

Sometimes the mere fact of changing from a poetic to a political context produces the satire or humour. What is praiseworthy in a poet—the ability to mingle fact and fiction skillfully (151)—becomes highly ironic when applied to a politician who

In Falsehood Probability imploys,
Nor his old Lies with newer Lies destroys.(p. 16)

Horace's "ut pictura poesis" (361) produces this bland but destructive couplet:

Not unlike Paintings, Principles appear,
Some best at distance, some when we are near. (p. 36)

More humourous than satirical is the relation between Horace's declaration that there's no place for a mediocre poet (372-73) and Bramston's

The Middle way the best we sometimes call.
But 'tis in Politicks no way at all.

There is no Medium: for the term in vogue
On either side is, Honest Man, or Rogue. (pp. 37-38)

The conclusion of the poem involves a somewhat more complex transformation. Horace closes with a humourously self-deprecating description of the "poetic itch": the afflicted poet stumbles into ditches as he babbles his verses aloud; people flee from him, and with good reason; if he catches anyone, he hangs on like a leech and reads his victim to death. Bramston describes another "sort of itch," parliamenteering. Sir Harry Clodpole knows better than to make speeches to the electors; he solicits their votes by feasting them, and they run *towards* him (or his table), not away. They, not he, are the leeches; "they never leave him while he's worth a groat" (p. 45).

Bramston—it seems an excessive refinement to speak of a persona or narrator—presents himself as a rather simple, naive political observer who yearns for clear-cut distinctions between parties; he wants to know where politicians stand on issues. The confusion, the blurring of old party lines, in present-day England is like the monster in the frontispiece. Though simple, he is also well informed. He seems to have a good knowledge of British history since the Restoration, referring casually to the Exclusion Crisis of 1680-81 (p. 15), the Kentish Petition of 1701 (p. 10), and the South Sea Bubble of 1720 (p. 7). All these past events are used to reinforce present lessons. He is up-to-date, as shown by his reference to the recent events in the careers of Methuen and Woolston. He professes familiarity with the characters of the leading politicians and also knows something about what is going on in the constituencies. He knows, or claims to know, how different kinds of listeners will react to different kinds of speeches.

For a son of Christ Church, one of the most Tory Colleges of Tory Oxford, he seems remarkably non-partisan, though his Opposition biases do show through. When he says that "Addison's immortal Page" shows us how "to screen good Ministers from Publick rage" (p. 9), he is clearly aiming at Walpole, known as the "Screenmaster General" since his success in shielding many of the perpetrators of the South Sea Bubble in 1720. (I have not been able to discover the passage of Addison that Bramston had in mind.) When the aspiring orator is urged not to "join with silver Tongue a brazen Face" (p. 24), Walpole is again present by innuendo, for "brazen-face" was another of his nicknames. On the

7

other hand, Bramston also makes fun of the "everlasting Fame" that results from quibbling on Sir Robert's name (p. 6). Bramston perhaps has it both ways here; while ridiculing commonplace puns, he also invites us to remember that "Robin" does indeed sound very much like "robbing."

Sometimes he is more subtle and ironic. This subtlety caused difficulty for at least one contemporary reader, and may do the same for us. Consider the following passage, which parallels Horace's advice always to show Achilles wrathful, Orestes mourning, and the like:

To *Likelihood* your *Characters* confine;
Don't turn *Sir Paul* out, let *Sir Paul* resign.
In *Walpole*'s Voice (if Factions Ill intend)
Give the two *Universities* a Friend;
Give *Maidston* Wit, and Elegance refin'd;
To both the *Pelhams* give the *Scipios* Mind;
To *Cart'ret*, Learning, Eloquence, and Parts;
To *George* the *Second*, give all *English* Hearts. (p. 13)

One of Bramston's early readers found his poem very faulty, and many of his complaints were directed against the passage just quoted.

Such artless art did ever mortal see,
Or politicks so void of policy?

What bard but this could Pelham's train compare
To Roman Scipio's thunder-bolts of war?
Did e'er their wars enrich their native isle,
With foreign treasures and with Spanish spoil?

But hark! and stare with all your ears and eyes!
Walpole is friend to Universities!

Hail politician bard! we ask not whether
A whig or tory; thou art both and neither.
Poultney and Walpole each adorn thy lays,
Which one for love, and one for money praise.
Alike are mention'd, equally are sung
Will. Shippen staunch, and slight Sir Wm. Young.
Bromley and Wyndham share the motley strain,
With Cart'ret, Maidstone, and the Pelhams twain.

This critic finds two main faults in the poem:
misinformation and confusion about particular individuals
and, more generally, an inability to distinguish Whigs from
Tories and give each their due. This last complaint of
course mocks Bramston's lament at the beginning of the
poem about the current lack of distinction between parties.

To what extent is this critique justified? What is Bramston
trying to do in this passage? There is no problem with the
second line: Sir Paul Methuen did indeed resign his office,
and one gets the impression from Hervey (pp. 101-2, 250)
that he never let anyone forget that he resigned. Thus we
have here the most conventional of truisms. Walpole is
more difficult. He was certainly no friend of the
universities, which were Tory hotbeds. On the other hand,
he was reluctant to try to reduce their privileges or bring
them more closely under government control, for fear of
rousing them to keener opposition. Nowhere else did he
follow so faithfully his policy of letting sleeping dogs lie.
In a certain sense, then, he might be called a friend of the
universities. I have been unable to determine whom
Bramston means by "Maidston"—perhaps one of the
Finches, the most prominent family in the area of

9

Maidstone, Kent. Bramston's critic is certainly right about
the Pelhams: they have nothing whatever in common with
the Scipios. Scipio Africanus Major (236-184/3) was one of
the most illustrious Roman heroes, consul during the
Second Punic War and an outstanding military tactician.
Scipio Africanus Minor (c. 185-129) was not only a consul
and a military hero but a great patron of letters whom
Cicero considered the greatest Roman of them all. Thomas
Pelham-Holles, Duke of Newcastle-upon-Tyne (1693-
1768), Walpole's chief election manager, was notoriously
muddle-headed, nervous, embarrassed, swamped in petty
detail, suspicious, fretful, pompous, and indecisive. His
brother, Henry Pelham (1695?-1754), was much less well
known; reserved and withdrawn, he preferred to work in
the background, and his tactical and organizational abilities
were not recognized until considerably later. As far as their
public image was concerned, then, no two men could be
less like the Scipios. Most contemporaries agreed with
Bramston's praise of John Carteret, Earl Granville (1690-
1763), though many of them also mention other, less
admirable traits. As for George II, it depends on whose
hearts you consult. An anonymous journalist:

What an Assurance has the Kingdom already given of an
unfeigned Affection to their Majesties Persons and
Government? How do the People shew that none are
acceptable to them, but those that are so to their Majesties?
How can Subjects give stronger Proofs of the high Esteem
they have their Sovereign in, for Penetration and Wisdom,
than those who entirely rely upon the Royal Discerning,
and regulate their Conduct by the King's Direction?

William Pultney:

The Queen is hated, the King despised, their son both the
one and the other, and such a spirit of disaffection to the

family and general discontent with the present Government is spread all over the Kingdom, that it is absolutely impossible for things to go on in the track they are now in.

By now Bramston's method should be clear: he is praising everyone, but the praise fits the Opposition (such as Carteret) much better than it does the Government (the Pelhams). There is perhaps room for doubt about Walpole and George II, but Bramston's critic's failure to see the irony in the comparison of Pelhams to Scipios must be the result of sheer obtuseness. The rationale for Bramston's technique becomes clearer if we look again at Horace and recall that the basis of his advice is to follow conventional opinion. The conventional opinions that Bramston is by implication urging his pupil to follow are those of the politician's supporters and dependents. It just happens that Bramston has chosen his examples so that the Opposition conventions are closer to reality than the Government conventions.

All this is fun, but it is quite inoffensive. There's no animus, no vehemence, no bite. Politics do not really engage any of Bramston's strong convictions. The self-portrait he offers us on pages 29-30 would be for many political satirists of the period a transparent facade of mock-innocence, but it seems to fit Bramston very accurately:

Alas Poor Me, you may my fortune guess: I write, and yet Humanity profess:

I love the King, the Queen, and Royal Race: I like the Government, but want no Place:

Was never in a Plot, my Brain's not hurt; I Politicks to Poetry convert.

By contrast to the increasing acrimony of most political satire of the late 1720's, this attitude is at least refreshing.

NOTES TO *THE ART OF POLITICKS*

Given the topical nature of *The Art of Politicks*, the best use of my remaining space is probably to annotate the poem. From what I have learned about its background—and many mysteries remain—I have tried to choose what seems most relevant. In the interests of saving space, and since full annotation is not possible anyway, I have kept documentation to a minimum, especially where the information comes from easily available sources like the DNB or, conversely, has been pieced together from several sources. Some works are occasionally referred to by abbreviation or author's name; the ones not mentioned in the Notes to the Introduction are the following:

Cobbett: William Cobbett, *The Parliamentary History of England from the Earliest Period to the Year 1803* (London: T. C. Hansard, 1806-20).

Ellis: Jonathan Swift, *A Discourse of the Contests and Dissentions between the Nobles and Commons in Athens and Rome*, ed. Frank H. Ellis (Oxford: Clarendon Press, 1967).

Grey: Anchitel Grey, *Debates of the House of Commons from the Year 1667 to the Year 1694* (London, 1763).

Thomas: Peter D. G. Thomas, *The House of Commons in the Eighteenth Century* (Oxford: Clarendon Press, 1971).

Realey: Charles B. Realey, *The Early Opposition to Sir Robert Walpole 1720-1727* (Lawrence: University of Kansas Press, 1931).

P. 1, line 1. Sir James: Sir James Thornhill (c. 1675-1734). As MP for Weymouth and Melcombe Regis (1722-34) and Serjeant Painter to the King (1720-32), he embodies the parallel between art and politics that underlies Bramston's poem. His best-known works were the dome of St. Paul's and the paintings in Greenwich Hospital. Hogarth married his daughter in 1729.

P. 2, line 4. Cf. Hervey's comment on Edmund Gibson, Bishop of London, who "affected to conciliate in himself both characters of Whig and Tory, declaring himself always a Whig in the State and a Tory in the Church" (pp. 90-91). Gibson's attitude can be traced back at least as far as Swift's *Sentiments of a Church of England Man* (1711).

line 11. Patriots: the self-awarded designation of the major group of Walpole's opponents.

P. 3, line 6. Parliament devoted considerable time to fixing turnpike tolls.

Fleury: André Hercule de (1653-1743). Created a cardinal in 1726, he was chief adviser to Louis XV of France from that date till his death, and therefore a person of great interest to England. His guiding principle was to keep France at peace with the rest of Europe.

P. 4, lines 2-3. "Tory" originally meant an Irish outlaw, and "Whig" a Scottish rebel. For other theories of the origin of "Whig" that were current in 1729, see OED.

line 12. Repetition Day: a day on which schoolboys recite memorized lessons.

P. 5, lines 7. The human face in Bramston's frontispiece has been said to resemble Heidegger, but it does not seem to match his reputation for extreme ugliness. See *TE*, 5, 92, 290, 443-44.

All Mr. Heydegger's *Letters come directed to him from abroad*, A Monsieur, Monsieur *Heydegger*, Surintendant des Plaisirs d' Angleterre.

P. 6, lines 3-4. Ridpath: George Ridpath (d. 1726), Whig journalist. Abel Roper (1665-1726), publisher of the *Tory Post Boy*.

P. 7, line 10. Pinkethman: William Pinkethman (or Penkethman) (d. 1725), a comic actor said to have once eaten three chickens in two seconds. See TE, 4, 220, 377.

line 12. Maypole: This remarkable barometer of intellectual history was razed by the Puritan parliament in 1644. A new one, 134 feet tall, was set up at the Restoration; it, or a successor, had decayed to a height of twenty feet in 1717 when Sir Isaac Newton acquired it and presented it to James Pound to use as a telescope mount.

P. 8, line 2. Newer Square: Cavendish Square, according to Horace Walpole's annotation.

line 6. The bridge at Putney Ferry was completed in 1729.

P. 9, lines 4-5. Thomas Tickell's poetical *Epistle from a Lady in England to a Gentleman at Avignon* went through five editions in 1717.

lines 6-7. "Caleb D'Anvers" was the pseudonym under which appeared *The Craftsman*, the opposition journal directed by Bolingbroke and Pultney. Bramston's expression of ignorance must be ironic.

P. 10, lines 1-2. Arthur Onslow, who became Speaker in 1728, insisted that all members bow to the Speaker's Chair when entering or leaving the House (Thomas, p. 356).

line 12. The "Kentish Petition" was presented to the Tory-controlled Parliament on 8 May 1701 by five gentlemen of Kent. It urged Parliament to grant speedily to King William the subsidies that would enable him to pursue his European wars against Louis XIV. Parliament did not consider its words soft; it voted the petition seditious, scandalous, and insolent, and arrested the five gentlemen, who thereupon became popular heroes, at least among the Whigs. See Defoe's *History of the Kentish Petition* (1701) and Ellis, pp. 53-56, 65-66.

P. 11, lines 3-8. Pultney: William Pultney (1684-1764), later Earl of Bath. The leader of the "Patriot" opposition to Walpole in the House of Commons. Hervey reluctantly concedes that his abilities were outstanding (pp. 790-91).

P. 12, line 4. the Rod: that is, the rod of the Serjeant-at-Arms, the officer responsible for keeping order in the House of Commons.

line 6. the Bar: The Bar marked the outer limit of the House, and, as the lines imply, was where offenders stood to be reprimanded.

lines 11-12. The "one cause" is presumably Walpole's patronage. The Cornish constituencies were notoriously corrupt even by eighteenth-century standards, and Walpole cultivated the Scots assiduously. A Scottish "laird" is a landowner, not a "lord" in the English sense.

P. 13, line 12. Flying-Squadron: apparently a group which claimed to vote by principle rather than from attachment to any party. Sir Joseph Jekyll was considered its leader. See Sedgwick, *House of Commons*, 2, 175; Realey, p. 54; and OED, "Squadron 7," "Squadrone b.," and "Squadronist."

P. 15, lines 2ff. The famous speech of Colonel Silius Titus (7 Jan. 1681) was widely reported in two slightly different versions; see Grey, 8, 279 and Cobbett, 4,1291. In both these versions the question is whether to keep the lion out or to let him in and chain him. Bramston may have been following an independent tradition or merely exercising poetic license. The lion is, of course, James, Duke of York, the Roman Catholic heir to the throne.

Lane: Sir Richard Lane (c. 1667-1756), MP for Worcester 1727-34. He was a merchant, sugar baker, and salt trader, and a consistent supporter of the administration. For examples of his indecorous use of biblical allusions see Sedgwick, 2, 197-98 (the "bantering speech" mentioned there used the Book of Revelation to prove that merchants were the best people on earth); and Knatchbull, p. 137.

P. 16, line 5. Rufus: King William II, son of William the Conqueror, known as William Rufus, was often evoked as an example of tyranny, as in Pope's *Windsor-Forest*.

P. 17, lines 9-10. Prince William: younger son of George II, eight years old in 1729; Louisa: youngest daughter of King George, then five.

P. 18, line 4. William Shippen (1673-1743) was an extreme Tory, noted for his outspoken attacks on the Walpole ministry, one of which landed him in the Tower. Sir William Yonge (c. 1693-1755) was notorious, at least among the opposition, for voluble but empty speeches in support of Walpole, "melodious nothings" as one satirist put it. See also Hervey, p. 36, and TE, 4, 394. The attack on *The Art of Politicks* quoted above complains that Shippen and Yonge should be mentioned in the same breath, but Bramston's point obviously is that the young MP cares nothing for either side.

P. 20, line 8. Polly Peachum is of course the heroine of Gay's *Beggar's Opera*. The role was played by Lavinia Fenton, who immediately became the toast of London. "Old Sir John" may be Sir John Hobart (1693-1756), although he was only fifteen years older than Miss Fenton (see Sedgwick, 2, 142). His name was sometimes spelled "Hubbard," and the following stanza appears in "A New Ballad Inscrib'd to Polly Peachum" (British Library C-116.i.4 #38), the cavalier typography of which perhaps indicates hasty composition:

Then came Sir J—— H— — Thundring at thy Cubboard: But you cast them like a Lubboard And did soon dispatch him.

Whoever he was, Sir John lost out to Charles Paulet, third Duke of Bolton, who kept Miss Fenton faithfully as his mistress, had three children by her, and married her on the death of his wife in 1751.

P. 21, line 10. The House of Commons had used St.Stephen's Chapel as its meeting place since the mid-sixteenth century. Dover-Court is "a proverbial term for a company, in which all are speakers and none hearers" (Bell).

P. 23, line 2. Waits: "a small body of wind instrumentalists maintained by a city or town at the public charge" (OED).

line 10. To sell bargains is to return indecent answers to civil questions.

P. 24, line 6. Mother Needham was a prominent bawd, notorious for her foul language. See TE, 4, 374-75, and 5, 293-94.

lines 7-8. "Oldfieldismus" and "Kibberismus" refer respectively to the styles of Anne Oldfield, a well-known actress, and Colley Cibber, playwright, stage manager, and hero of the *Dunciad*. Mrs. Oldfield was generally respected, but Pope, like Bramston, seems to have disliked her (TE, 4, 375).

line 11. Tallboy was a booby young lover in Richard Brome's comedy *The Jovial Crew* (1641), popular throughout the eighteenth century.

P. 26, line 12. Mist: Nathaniel Mist, Tory journalist. See TE, 5, 448. Eusden: Laurence Eusden, Poet Laureate 1718-30, often ridiculed by Pope.

line 14. Cibber's opera is *Love in a Riddle* (1729), designed to capitalize on the craze for ballad opera created by *The Beggar's Opera*.

P. 27, line 5. Censor: Sir Richard Steele as Isaac Bickerstaffe, the nominal author of *The Tatler*.

P. 29, line 6. Where Edmund Curll stood was in the pillory.

P. 31, line 3. Hugo Grotius's classic of political science, *De jure belli ac pacis*, was published in 1625 and translated in 1654.

P. 32, line 1. Wickfort: Abraham de Wicquefort, *l'Ambassadeur et ses fonctions* (La Haye, 1680). It was summarized in *The Craftsman* of 23 Sept. 1727.

    line 4. John Banks was the author of *The Unhappy Favourite; or the Earl of Essex* (1681) and of *The Island Queens, or the Death of Mary, Queen of Scotland* (prohibited in 1684; a revision was produced in 1704). Bell says that although "written in the most contemptible language, yet they never fail to melt the audience into tears, merely by the force of judicious and well-arranged plots and incidents."

P. 33, line 1. Arch-Bishop: William Wake, Archbishop of Canterbury since 1716. He was 72 in 1729. Master of the Rolls: Sir Joseph Jekyll, who had held the office since 1717, was about 66 in 1729.

    line 12. Spence: Thomas Spence (d. 1737), Serjeant-at-Arms.

P. 34, line 3. Toft: In 1726 one Mary Toft claimed to have given birth to seventeen live rabbits, and some who should have known better believed her. See Pope's poem on her, *TE*, 6, 259, and Hogarth's engraving.

throws: i.e., throes, labor pains.

    line 8. Bromley and Hanmer: William Bromley (?1663-1732), MP for Oxford 1701-32, Speaker 1710-13; Sir Thomas Hanmer (1677-1746), who represented several constituencies from 1701-27 and was Speaker 1714-15. They were Tory heroes, at least to Atterbury, for having refused the places offered them by George I in 1715 (Foord, p. 51).

P. 35, line 1. Tonson: Jacob Tonson, prominent bookseller.

line 9. Cler. Dom. Com.: "Clerk of the House of Commons."

P. 36, line 2. Die Martis is Tuesday; Thursday is Die Jovis.

line 6. Wyndham: Sir William Wyndham, MP for Somerset 1710-40, prominent opposition leader from the 1720s. See Sedgwick, 2, 562-64, for his reputation. Hervey believed that his high reputation was partly due to Walpole's henchmen, who inflated it in order to deflate Pultney's (p. 21).

P. 44, line 4. Sir Robert Fagg was better known for horse-racing and wenching than for politics; he appears in Hogarth's painting of *The Beggar's Opera* admiring Lavinia Fenton and in the ballad cited in my note to p. 20, line 8. Running for Parliament in the borough of Steyning, Sussex, in 1722, he came in third in a five-man race with nineteen votes. He also ran third in 1727; the vote is not recorded, unless Bramston's "two Voices" is to be taken literally.

Université de Montréal

NOTES TO THE INTRODUCTION

Letter to John Caryll, 6 Feb. 1731. *Correspondence*, ed. George Sherburn (Oxford: Clarendon Press, 1956), 3, 173.

See also Antony Coleman's introduction to James Miller's *Harlequin-Horace* (1731; ARS 178).

D. F. Foxon, *English Verse 1701-1750* (Cambridge: The University Press, 1975), 1, 77. I should also like to thank Mr. Foxon for generous personal help.

I owe my knowledge of Bell's edition to Kent Mullikin of the University of North Carolina.

Woolston was convicted on four counts of blasphemy on 4 March 1729. His offending works were six *Discourses on the Miracles of our Saviour* (1727-29). He never succeeded in paying his fine of £100 (Pope, *Poems* (Twickenham Edition, genl. ed. John Butt; London: Methuen, New Haven: Yale University Press, 1939-69), 5, 459). Hereafter referred to as *TE*.

Methuen's resignation is erroneously dated in 1730 in *DNB* and in Romney Sedgwick, *The House of Commons 1715-1754* (New York: Oxford University Press, 1970), 2, 254. See Abel Boyer, *The Political State of Great Britain, 37* (May 1729), 523, and John, Lord Hervey. *Some Materials towards Memoirs of the Reign of King George II*, ed. Romney Sedgwick (London: Eyre and Spottiswoode, 1931), pp. 101-02. According to Hervey, Methuen's ostensible reason for resigning was his dislike of the general conduct of the court, his real reason his failure to be appointed Secretary of State.

Translations of Horace are taken from the Loeb Library edition, trans. H. Rushton Fairclough (Cambridge, Mass., Harvard University Press, 1961). Line numbers of the Latin verse are in the text.

"Verses on the Art of Politicks," *Additions to the Works of Alexander Pope, Esq. Together with Many Original Poems and Letters, of Contemporary Writers, Never Before Published* (London, 1776). 1. 158-59. I have been unable to discover where the poem was first printed.

J. H. Plumb. *Sir Robert Walpole* (London: Cresset). Vol. I (1956). pp. 249-50; Sir Edward Knatchbull, *Parliamentary*

Diary, 1722-30, ed. A. N. Newman (London: Offices of the Royal Historical Society, 1963), p.42.

Most of my information about the Scipios comes from the *Oxford Companion to Classical Literature*.

DNB; Ray A. Kelch, *Newcastle: A Duke without Money* (Berkeley and Los Angeles: University of California Press, 1974), pp. 9-11; Reed Browning, *The Duke of Newcastle* (New Haven and London: Yale University Press, 1975), pp. xi-xiii, 80-88.

DNB; Browning, p. 18.

Plumb, *Walpole, 2* (1960), 52-53; Hervey, pp. 411-12; Browning, p. 113; Archibald S. Foord, *His Majesty's Opposition, 1714-1830* (Oxford: Clarendon Press, 1964), pp. 142-45.

The British Journal, 258 (2 Sept. 1727), p. 1.

Reported by Hervey toward the end of 1729 (p. 105).

For illuminating discussions of Opposition ideology and literary strategies, see Maynard Mack, *The Garden and the City: Retirement and Politics in the Later Poetry of Pope, 1731-1743* (Toronto and Buffalo: University of Toronto Press, 1969); Isaac Kramnick, *Bolingbroke and his Circle: The Politicks of Nostalgia in the Age of Walpole* (Cambridge: Harvard University Press, 1968); and J.V. Guerinot and Rodney D. Jilg, eds., *The Beggar's Opera: Contexts* (Hamden, Conn.: Archon Books, 1976), esp. pp. 69-95.

Part of the research for this introduction was done while I held a Leave Fellowship from the Canada Council, whom I should like to thank for their support.

BIBLIOGRAPHICAL NOTE

The facsimile of *The Art of Politicks* (1729) is reproduced by permission from a copy of the first edition (Shelf Mark: *PR3326/B287A8; Foxon B383) in the William Andrews Clark Memorial Library. The total type-page (p. 19) measures 152 x 93 mm.

THE
ART of POLITICKS,
In Imitation of
HORACE's
ART of POETRY.

THE
ART of POLITICKS,
In Imitation of
HORACE's
ART of POETRY.

OF to a Human Face Sir *James* should draw
    A Gelding's Mane, and Feathers of Maccaw,
    A Lady's Bosom, and a Tail of Cod,
Who could help laughing at a Sight so odd?
 Just such a Monster, Sirs, pray think before ye,
When you behold one Man both *Whig* and *Tory*.
Not more extravagant are Drunkard's Dreams,
Than *Low-Church* Politicks with *High-Church* Schemes.
Painters, you'll say, may their own Fancies use,
And Freeborn *Britons* may their *Party* chuse;
That's true, I own: but can one Piece be drawn
For Dove and Dragon, Elephant and Fawn?
 Speakers profess'd, who Gravity pretend,   )
With motley Sentiments their Speeches blend:)
Begin like Patriots , and like Courtiers end.)

Some love to roar, *the Constitution's broke*,
And others on the *Nation's Debts* to joke;
Some rail, (they hate a Commonwealth so much,)
What e'er the Subject be, against the *Dutch*;
While others, with more fashionable Fury,
Begin with *Turnpikes*, and conclude with *Fleury*;
Some, when th' Affair was *Blenheim*'s glorious Battle,
Declaim'd against importing *Irish Cattle*.
But you, from what e'er Side you take your Name,
Like *Anna*'s *Motto*, always be the same.
  Outsides deceive, 'tis hard the Truth to know;)
Parties from quaint Denominations flow,)
As *Scotch* and *Irish* Antiquaries show.)
The *Low* are said to take Fanaticks Parts,
The *High* are bloody *Papists* in their Hearts.
Caution and Fear to highest Faults have run;
In pleasing both the Parties, you please none.
Who in the *House* affects declaiming Airs,
Whales in *Change-Alley* paints: in *Fish-Street, Bears*.
Some Metaphors, some Handkerchiefs display;)
These peep in Hats, while those with Buttons play,)
And make me think it *Repetition-Day*;)
 There Knights haranguing hug a neighb'ring Post,
And are but *Quorum* Orators at most.
Sooner than thus my want of Sense expose,)
I'd deck out Bandy-Legs with Gold-Clock't Hose,)
Or wear a Toupet-Wig without a Nose.)
Nay, I would sooner have thy Phyz, I swear,
Surintendant des Plaisirs d' Angleterre.
 Ye *Weekly Writers* of seditious *News*,
Take Care your *Subjects* artfully to chuse,
Write *Panegyrick* strong, or boldly *rail*,
You cannot miss *Preferment*, or a *Goal*.
 Wrap up your Poison well, nor fear to say
What was a Lye last Night is Truth to Day;
Tell this, sink that, arrive at *Ridpath*'s Praise,

Let *Abel Roper* your Ambition raise.
To Lye fit Opportunity observe,
Saving some double Meaning in reserve;
But oh, you'll merit everlasting Fame,
If you can quibble on Sir *Robert*'s Name.
In *State-Affairs* use not the Vulgar Phrase,
Talk Words scarce known in good Queen *Besse*'s days.
New Terms let War or Traffick introduce,
And try to bring *Persuading Ships* in Use.
 Coin Words: in coining ne'er mind common Sense,
Provided the Original be *French*.
 Like *South-Sea Stock*, Expressions rise and fall:
King *Edward*'s Words are now no Words at all.
Did ought your Predecessors Genius cramp?
Sure ev'ry Reign may have it's proper Stamp.
All Sublunary things of Death partake;
What Alteration does a Cent'ry make?
Kings and Comedians all are mortal found,
Cæsar and *Pinkethman* are under Ground.
What's not destroy'd by Times devouring Hand?
Where's *Troy*, and where's the *May-Pole* in the *Strand*?
 Pease, Cabbages, and Turnips once grew, where
Now stands new *Bond-street*, and a newer Square;
Such Piles of Buildings now rise up and down;
London itself seems going out of *Town*.
Our Fathers cross'd from *Fulham* in a Wherry,
Their Sons enjoy a Bridge at *Putney-Ferry*.
Think we that modern Words eternal are?
Toupet, and *Tompion*, *Cosins*, and *Colmar*
Hereafter will be call'd by some plain Man
A *Wig*, a *Watch*, a *Pair of Stays*, a *Fan*.
To Things themselves if Time such change affords,
Can there be any trusting to our Words.
 To screen good Ministers from Publick rage,)
And how with Party Madness to engage,)
We learn from *Addison*'s immortal Page.)

The *Jacobite*'s ridiculous Opinion
Is seen from *Tickel*'s Letter to *Avignon*.
But who puts *Caleb*'s *Country-Craftsman* out,
Is still a secret, and the World's in doubt.
 Not long since *Parish-Clerks*, with saucy airs,
Apply'd *King David*'s *Psalms* to *State-Affairs*.
Some certain *Tunes* to Politicks belong,
On both Sides Drunkards love a Party-Song.
  If full a-cross the Speaker's Chair I go,
Can I be said the *Rules* o'th' *House* to know?
I'll ask, nor give offence without intent,
Nor through meer Sheepishness be impudent.
 In *Acts of Parliament* avoid Sublime,
Nor e'er Address his Majesty in Rhime;
An *Act of Parliament*'s a serious thing,
Begins with Year of Lord and Year of King;
Keeps close to Form, in every word is strict,
When it would *Pains* and *Penalties* inflict.
Soft Words suit best *Petitioners* intent;
Soft Words, O ye *Petitioners* of Kent!
  Who e'er harangues before he gives his Vote,
Should send sweet Language from a tuneful Throat.
Pultney the coldest Breast with Zeal can fire,
And *Roman Thoughts* by *Attick Stile* inspire;
He knows from tedious Wranglings to beguile
The serious *House* into a chearful Smile;
When the great Patriot paints his anxious Fears
For *England*'s Safety, I am lost in Tears.
But when dull Speakers strive to move compassion,
I pity their poor Hearers, not the Nation:
Unless young *Members* to the purpose speak,
I fall a laughing, or I fall asleep.
  Can Men their inward Faculties controul?
Is not the Tongue an Index to the Soul?
Laugh not in time of *Service* to your God,
Nor bully, when in *Custody* o'th' *Rod*;

Look Grave, and be from Jokes and Grinning far,
When brought to sue for Pardon at the *Bar*.
If then you let your ill-tim'd Wit appear,
Knights, Citizens, and Burgesses will sneer.
 For Land, or Trade, not the same Notions sire
The *City-Merchant*, and the *Country-Squire*;
Their Climes are distant, tho' one Cause unites
The *Lairds* of *Scotland*, and the *Cornish Knights*.
 To *Likelihood* your *Characters* confine;
Don't turn *Sir Paul* out, let *Sir Paul* resign.
In *Walpole*'s Voice (if Factions Ill intend)
Give the Two *Universities* a Friend;
Give *Maidston* Wit, and Elegance refin'd;
To both the *Pelhams* give the *Scipios* Mind;
To *Cart'ret*, Learning, Eloquence, and Parts;
To *George* the *Second*, give all *English* Hearts.
 Sometimes fresh Names in Politicks produce,
And Factions yet unheard of introduce;
And if you dare attempt a thing so new,
Make to itself the *Flying-Squadron* true.
 To speak is free, no *Member* is debarr'd:
But *Funds* and *National Accounts* are hard:
Safer on common Topicks to discourse,
The *Malt-Tax*, and a *Military Force*.
On these each Coffee-House will lend a hint,
Besides a thousand things that are in Print.
But steal not Word for Word, nor Thought for Thought:
For you'll be teaz'd to death, if you are caught.
When Factious Leaders boast increasing strength,
Go not too far, nor follow ev'ry Length:
Leave room for Change, turn with a grace about,
And swear you left 'em, when you found 'em out,
 With Art and Modesty your Part maintain:
And talk like *Col'nel Titus*, not like *Lane*;
The Trading-Knight with Rants his Speech begins,
Sun, Moon, and Stars, and Dragons, Saints, and Kings:

But *Titus* said, with his uncommon Sense,
When the *Exclusion-Bill* was in suspense,
I hear a Lyon in the Lobby roar;
Say, Mr. Speaker, shall we shut the door
And keep him there, or shall we let him in
To try if we can turn him out again?
 Some mighty Blusterers *Impeach* with noise,
And call their Private Cry, the Nation's Voice;
  From Folio's of Accounts they take their handles,
And the whole Ballance proves a pound of Candles;
As if *Paul*'s Cupola were brought to bed,
After hard Labour, of a small Pin's Head.
 Some *Rufus*, some the *Conqueror* bring in,
And some from *Julius Cæsar*'s days begin.
A cunning Speaker can command his chaps,
And when the *House* is not in humour, stops;
In Falsehood Probability imploys,
Nor his old Lies with newer Lies destroys.
  If when you speak, you'd hear a Needle fall,
And make the frequent *hear-hims* rend the wall,
In matters suited to your Taste engage,
Remembring still your Quality and Age.
Thy task be this, young Knight, and hear my Song
What Politicks to ev'ry Age belong.
 When *Babes* can speak, *Babes* should be taught to say,
King George the Second's Health, Huzza, Huzza!
Boys should learn *Latin* for *Prince William*'s sake,
And Girls *Louisa* their Example make.
  More loves the *Youth*, just come to his Estate,
To range the fields, than in the *House* debate;
More he delights in fav'rite Jowler's Tongue,
Than in *Will Shippen*, or *Sir William Yong*:
If in one Chase he can two Horses kill,
He cares not twopence for the Land-Tax Bill:
Loud in his Wine, in Women not o'er nice,
He damns his Uncles if they give advice;

Votes as his Father did, when there's a *Call*,
But had much rather, never Vote at all.
  We take a diff'rent Turn at *Twenty-six*,
And lofty thoughts on some Lord's Daughter fix;
With Men in Pow'r strict Friendship we persue,
With some considerable Post in view.
A Man of *Forty* fears to change his Note,
One way to Speak, and t'other way to Vote;
Careful his Tongue in Passion to command,
Avoids the Bar, and Speaker's Reprimand.
 In Bags the *Old Man* lets his Treasure rust,
Afraid to use it, or the Funds to trust;
When Stocks are low, he wants the heart to buy,
And through much caution sees 'em rise too high;
 Thinks nothing rightly done since *Seventy-eight*,
Swears present *Members* do not talk, but prate:
In *Charles the Second*'s days, says he, ye Prigs,
Torys were *Torys* then, and *Whigs* were *Whigs*.
Alas! this is a lamentable Truth,
We lose in age, as we advance in youth:
I laugh, when twenty will like eighty talk,
And old *Sir John* with *Polly Peachum* walk.
 Now as to *Double*, or to *False Returns*,
When pockets suffer, and when anger burns,
O Thing surpassing faith! Knight strives with Knight,
When both have brib'd, and neither's in the right.
 The Bayliff's self is sent for in that case,
And all the Witnesses had face to face.
Selected *Members* soon the fraud unfold,
In full Committee of the *House* 'tis told;
Th' incredible Corruption is destroy'd,
The Chairman's angry, and th' Election void.
 Those who would captivate the well-bred throng,
Should not too often speak, nor speak too long:
Church, nor Church Matters ever turn to Sport,
Nor make *St. Stephen's Chappel*, *Dover-Court*.

The *Speaker*, when the Commons are assembl'd,
May to the *Græcian Chorus* be resembl'd;
'Tis his the Young and Modest to espouse,
And see none draw, or challenge in the *House*:
'Tis his Old Hospitality to use,
And three good Printers for the *House* to chuse;
To let each Representative be heard,
And take due care the *Chaplain* be preferr'd,
To hear no *Motion* made that's out of joint,
And where he spies his *Member*, make his point.
 To Knights new chosen in old time would come
The *County Trumpet*, and perhaps a *Drum*;
Now when a Burgess new Elect appears,
Come Trainbands, Horseguards, Footguards, Grenadeers;
 When the majority the Town-clerk tells,
His Honour pays the Fiddles, Waits, and Bells:
Harangues the *Mob*, and is as wise and great,
As the most Mystic Oracle of State.
 When the Duke's Grandson for the County stood,
His Beef was fat, and his October good;
His Lordship took each Ploughman by the fist,
Drunk to their Sons, their Wives and Daughters kiss'd;
But when strong Beer their Freeborn Hearts inflames,
They sell him Bargains, and they call him Names.
Thus is it deem'd in *English* Nobles wise
To stoop for no one reason but to rise.
 Election matters shun with cautious awe,
O all ye Judges Learned in the Law;
A Judge by Bribes as much himself degrades,
As Dutchess Dowager by Masquerades.
 Try not with Jests obscene to force a Smile,
Nor lard your Speech with Mother *Needham*'s Stile:
Let not your tongue to Ωλδφιελδισμυς run,
And Κιββερισμυς with abhorrence shun;
Let not your looks affected words disgrace,
Nor join with silver Tongue a brazen Face;

Let not your hands, like Tallboys, be employ'd,
And the mad rant of Tragedy avoid.
 Just in your Thoughts, in your Expression clear,
Neither too modest, nor too bold appear.
 Others in vain a like Success will boast,
He speaks most easy, who has study'd most.
 A Peer's pert Heir has to the Commons spoke
A vile Reflection, or a Bawdy Joke;
Call'd to the House of Lords, of this beware,
'Tis what the *Bishops Bench* will never bear.
Amongst the *Commons* is such freedom shown,
They lash each other, and attack the Throne:
Yet so unskilful or so fearful some,
For nine that speak there's nine-and-forty dumb.
 When *James* the *first*, at great *Britannia*'s helm,
Rul'd this word-clipping and word-coining Realm,
No words to Royal favour made pretence,
But what agreed in sound and clash'd in sense.
Thrice happy he! how great that Speaker's praise,
Whose ev'ry Period look'd an hundred ways.
What then? we now with just abhorrence shun
The trifling Quibble, and the School-boys Pun;
Tho' no great Connoisseur, I make a shift
Just to find out a *Durfey* from a *Swift*;
I can discern with half an eye, I hope,
Mist from *Jo Addison*, from *Eusden Pope*:
I know a Farce from one of *Congreve*'s Plays,
And *Cibber*'s Opera from *Johnny Gay*'s.
 When pert *Defoe* his sawcy Papers writ,
He from a Cart was Pillor'd for his Wit:
By Mob was pelted half a Morning's space,
And rotten Eggs besmear'd his yellow face;
The *Censor* then improv'd the list'ning Isle,
And held both Parties in an artful Smile.
A Scribbling Crew now pinching Winter brings,)
That spare no earthly nor no heav'nly things,)

Nor Church, nor State, nor Treasurers, nor Kings.)
But Blasphemy displeases all the Town;)
And for defying Scripture, Law, and Crown,)
Woolston should pay his Fine, and lose his Gown,)
  It must be own'd the *Journals* try all ways
To merit their respective Party's praise:
They jar in every Article from *Spain*;
A War these threaten, those a Peace maintain:
Tho' Lye they will, to give 'em all their due,
In Foreign matters, and Domestick too.
Whoe'er thou art that would'st a *Postman* write,
Enquire all day, and hearken all the night.
Sure, *Gazetteers* and Writers of *Courants*
Might soon exceed th' Intelligence of *France*:
To be out-done old *England* should refuse,
As in her Arms, so in her Publick News;
But Truth is scarce, the Scene of Action large,
And Correspondence an excessive Charge.
  There are who say, no Man can be a Wit
Unless for *Newgate* or for *Bedlam* fit;
Let Pamphleteers abusive Satyr write,
To shew a Genius is to shew a Spite:
That Author's Works will ne'er be reckon'd good
Who has not been where *Curl* the Printer stood.
 Alass Poor Me, you may my fortune guess:
I write, and yet Humanity profess;
(Tho' nothing can delight a modern Judge,
Without ill-nature and a private Grudge)
I love the King, the Queen, and Royal Race:
I like the Government, but want no Place:
 Too low in Life to be a *Justice* I,
And for a Constable, thank God, too high;
Was never in a Plot, my Brain's not hurt;
I Politicks to Poetry convert.
 A Politician must (as I have read)
Be furnish'd, in the first place, with a *Head*:

A *Head* well fill'd with *Machiavelian* Brains,
And stuff'd with Precedents of former Reigns:
Must Journals read, and *Magna Charta* quote;
But acts still wiser, if he speaks by *Note*:
Learns well his Lesson, and ne'er fears mistakes:
For Ready Money Ready Speakers makes;
He must Instructions and Credentials draw,
Pay well the Army, and protect the Law:
 Give to his Country what's his Country's due,
But first help *Brothers*, *Sons*, and *Cousins* too.
He must read *Grotius* upon War and Peace,
And the twelve Judges Salary encrease.
He must oblige old Friends and new Allies,
And find out *Ways and Means* for fresh *Supplies*.
He must the Weavers Grievances redress,
And Merchants wants in Merchants words express.
 Dramatick Poets that expect the Bays,
Should cull our Histories for Party Plays;
 Wickfort's Embassador should fill their head,
And the *State-Tryals* carefully be read:
For what is *Dryden*'s Muse and *Otway*'s Plots
To th' *Earl of Essex* or the *Queen of Scots*?
 'Tis said that *Queen Elizabeth* could speak,
At twelve years old, right *Attick* full-mouth'd *Greek*;
Hence was the Student forc'd at *Greek* to drudge,
If he would be a Bishop, or a Judge.
Divines and Lawyers now don't think they thrive,
'Till promis'd places of men still alive:
How old is such an one in such a Post?
The answer is, he's seventy-five almost:
 Th' Arch-Bishop, and the Master of the Rolls?
Neither is young, and one's as old as *Paul*'s.
Will Men, that ask such Questions, publish books
Like learned *Hooker*'s or *Chief Justice Cook*'s?
 On Tender Subjects with discretion touch,
And never say too little, or too much.

On Trivial Matters Flourishes are wrong,
Motions for Candles never should be long:
Or if you move, in case of sudden Rain,
To shut the Windows, speak distinct and plain.
Unless you talk good *English* downright Sense,
Can you be understood by Serjeant *Spence*?
  New Stories always should with Truth agree
Or Truth's half-Sister, Probability:
Scarce could *Toft*'s Rabbits and pretended throws
On half the Honourable *House* impose.
  When *Cato* speaks, young *Shallow* runs away,
And swears it is so dull he cannot stay:
When Rakes begin on Blasphemy to border,
Bromley and *Hanmer* cry aloud—— *To Order*.
The point is this, with manly Sense and ease
T' inform the Judgment, and the Fancy please.
Praise it deserves, nor difficult the thing,
At once to serve one's Countrey and one's King.
  Such Speeches bring the wealthy *Tonson*'s gain,)
From Age to Age they minuted remain,)
As Precedents for *George* the twentieth's Reign.)
  Is there a Man on earth so perfect found,
Who ne'er mistook a word in Sense or Sound?
Not Blund'ring, but persisting is the fault;
No mortal Sin is *Lapsus Linguæ* thought:
Clerks may mistake; consid'ring who 'tis from,
I pardon little Slips in *Cler. Dom. Com.*
  But let me tell you I'll not take his part,
If ev'ry *Thursday* he date *Die Mart.*
Of Sputt'ring mortals 'tis the fatal curse,
By mending Blunders still to make 'em worse.
Men sneer when—— gets a lucky Thought,
And stare if *Wyndham* should be nodding caught.
But sleeping's what the wisest men may do,
Should the Committee chance to sit 'till Two.

Not unlike Paintings, Principles appear,
Some best at distance, some when we are near.
The love of Politicks so vulgar's grown,
My Landlord's Party from his Sign is known:
 Mark of *French* wine, see *Ormond*'s Head appear,
While *Marlb'rough*'s Face directs to Beer and Beer:
Some *Buchanan*'s, the *Pope*'s Head some like best,
The *Devil Tavern* is a standing jest.
 Whoe'er you are that have a Seat secure,
Duly return'd, and from *Petition* sure,
Stick to your Friends in whatsoe'er you say;
With strong aversion shun the Middle way:
The Middle way the best we sometimes call,
But 'tis in Politicks no way at all.
A *Trimmer*'s what both Parties turn to sport,
By Country hated, and despis'd at Court.
 Who would in earnest to a Party come,
Must give his Vote, not whimsical, but plumb.
There is no Medium: for the term in vogue
On either side is, Honest Man, or Rogue.
Can it be difficult our Minds to show,
Where all the Difference is, Yes, or No?
 In all Professions, Time and Pains give Skill,
Without hard Study, dare Physicians kill?
Can he that ne'er read Statutes or Reports,
Give Chamber-Counsel, or urge Law in Courts?
But ev'ry Whipster knows Affairs of State,
Nor fears on nicest Subjects to debate.
 A Knight of eighteen hundred pounds a year—
Who minds his Head, if his Estate be clear?
Sure he may speak his mind, and tell the *House*,
He matters not the Government a Louse.
Lack-learning Knights, these things are safely said
To Friends in private, at the *Bedford-Head*:
But in the *House*, before your Tongue runs on,
Consult *Sir James*, *Lord William*'s dead and gone.

Words to recall is in no Member's power,
One single word may send you to the *Tower*.
 The wrong'd to help, the lawless to restrain,
Thrice ev'ry Year, in ancient *Egbert*'s Reign,
 The *Members* to the *Mitchelgemot* went,
In after Ages call'd the *Parliament*;
Early the *Mitchelgemot* did begin
T' enroll their Statutes, on a Parchment Skin:
For impious Treason hence no room was left,
For Murder, for Polygamy, or Theft:
Since when the Senates power both Sexes know
From Hops and Claret, Soap and Callico.
Now wholesom Laws young Senators bring in
'Gainst *Goals*, *Attornies*, *Bribery*, and *Gin*.
Since such the nature of the *British* State,
 The power of *Parliament* so old and great,
Ye 'Squires and *Irish* Lords, 'tis worth your care)
To be return'd for City, Town, or Shire,)
By Sheriff, Bailiff, Constable, or Mayor.)
 Some doubt, which to a Seat has best Pretence,
A man of Substance, or a man of Sense:
But never any Member feats will do,
Without a Head-piece and a Pocket too;
Sense is requir'd the depth of Things to reach,
And Money gives Authority to Speech.
 A Man of Bus'ness won't 'till ev'ning dine;
Abstains from Women, Company, and Wine:
 From *Fig*'s new Theatre he'll miss a Night,
Tho' Cocks, and Bulls, and *Irish* Women fight:
Nor sultry Sun, nor storms of soaking Rain,
The Man of Bus'ness from the *House* detain:
Nor speaks he for no reason but to say,
I am a *Member*, and I spoke to day.
I speak sometimes, you'll hear his Lordship cry,
Because Some speak that have less Sense than I.

The Man that has both Land and Money too
May wonders in a Trading Borough do:
They'll praise his Ven'son, and commend his Port,)
Turn their two former Members into Sport,)
And, if he likes it, Satyrize the Court.)
 But at a Feast 'tis difficult to know
From real Friends an undiscover'd Foe;
The man that swears he will the Poll secure,
And pawns his Soul that your Election's sure,
Suspect that man: beware, all is not right,
He's, ten to one, a Corporation-Bite.
 Alderman *Pond*, a downright honest Man,
Would say, I cannot help you, or I can:
To spend your Money, Sir, is all a jest;
Matters are settled, set your heart at rest:
We've made a Compromise, and, Sir, you know,
That sends one Member *High*, and t'other *Low*.
 But if his good Advice you would not take,
He'd scorn your Supper, and your Punch forsake:
Leave you of mighty Interest to brag,
And poll two Voices like *Sir Robert Fag*.
 Parliamenteering is a sort of Itch,
That will too oft unwary Knights bewitch.
Two good Estates Sir *Harry Clodpole* spent;
Sate thrice, but spoke not once, in Parliament:
Two good Estates are gone—Who'll take his word?
Oh! should his Uncle die, he'd spend a third:
He'd buy a House, his happiness to crown,
Within a mile of some good *Borough-Town*;
 Tag, Rag, and Bobtail to Sir *Harry*'s run,
Men that have Votes, and Women that have none:
Sons, Daughters, Grandsons, with his Honour dine;
He keeps a Publick-House without a Sign.
Coolers and Smiths extol th' ensuing Choice,
And drunken Taylors boast their right of Voice.
Dearly the free-born neighbourhood is bought,

They never leave him while he's worth a groat:
So Leeches stick, nor quit the bleeding wound,
Till off they drop with Skinfuls to the ground.

FINIS.